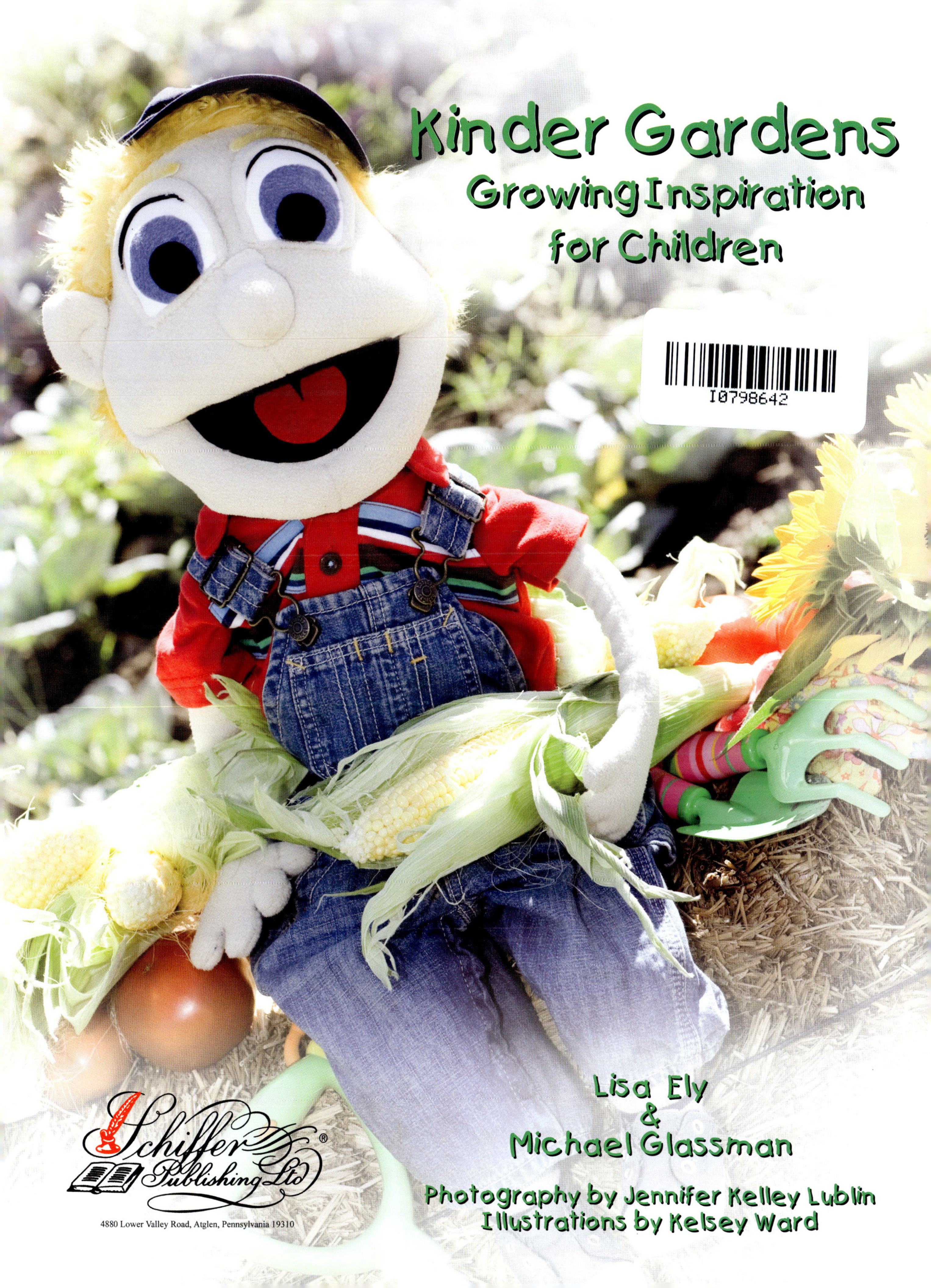

Kinder Gardens

Growing Inspiration for Children

Lisa Ely
&
Michael Glassman

Photography by Jennifer Kelley Lublin
Illustrations by Kelsey Ward

Schiffer Publishing Ltd®
4880 Lower Valley Road, Atglen, Pennsylvania 19310

Lisa Ely, at age 5, planting her first garden with her daddy.

Dedication

I dedicate this book to my husband Ryan, without whose help, love, and support this book would never have been finished, and to my kids, Cameron and Ripken, who are my greatest achievements. Thank you all for your inspirations and always being willing to get your hands dirty!

Lisa Ely

I dedicate this book to my daughter, Jordan, who always inspires me and makes me a better father and a better man.

Michael Glassman

Other Schiffer Books on Related Schiffer Books:

Children's Playhouses: Plans & Ideas. Tina Skinner
ISBN: 0-7643-1416-5 • $29.95

Soap Carving for Children of All Ages. Howard K. Suzuki
ISBN: 0-7643-0859-9 • $12.95

Library of Congress Control Number: 2009942137

Type set in Kids/Zurich BT/ Impress BT
Designed by Tina Skinner and Stephanie Daugherty
ISBN: 978-0-7643-3453-5
Printed in China

Schiffer Books are available at special discounts for bulk purchases for sales promotions or premiums. Special editions, including personalized covers, corporate imprints, and excerpts can be created in large quantities for special needs. For more information contact the publisher:

Schiffer Publishing Ltd.
4880 Lower Valley Road
Atglen, PA 19310
Phone: (610) 593-1777; Fax: (610) 593-2002
E-mail: Info@schifferbooks.com

For the largest selection of fine reference books on this and related subjects, please visit our web site at *www.schifferbooks.com*
We are always looking for people to write books on new and related subjects. If you have an idea for a book please contact us at the above address.

This book may be purchased from the publisher. Include $5.00 for shipping. Please try your bookstore first. You may write for a free catalog.

In Europe, Schiffer books are distributed by
Bushwood Books
6 Marksbury Ave.
Kew Gardens
Surrey TW9 4JF England
Phone: 44 (0) 20 8392 8585; Fax: 44 (0) 20 8392 9876
E-mail: info@bushwoodbooks.co.uk
Website: www.bushwoodbooks.co.uk

How adult helpers can use this book

Everyone who has a child or works with children has been faced with the difficulty of getting them to eat their vegetables. Well, when children grow their own vegetables you see a whole new attitude toward eating them. They will become extremely proud and will not want to wait until the next veggie is ready to pick and eat.

Kids and gardening just go together. You have dirt, water, bugs, and food: what else could you ask for? The trick to gardening with kids is to make "gardening" a fun word and not an icky chore word.

The key is to start kids off as early as possible and get them excited about gardening in general. You'll not only be growing plants, you'll be growing fun.

This book is not about the science of how plants grow. It is more about getting them to get their hands dirty first, then teaching them about how things grow. We hope this book will inspire you to get your hands dirty and see the benefits of growing your own food. We love that healthy growing leads to healthy eating habits.

There is a new resurgence in sustainability, going green, and appreciating Mother Earth. It is time to introduce children to the joys and wonders of growing their own food. Children, especially those who live in the inner city, seem to have a severe disconnect about understanding where food actually comes from. We want to help you teach them.

The time you spend with your children as a family is priceless, and creating those memories in the garden, big or small, is definitely worth its weight in vegetables.

Table of Contents

Section 1

Getting Started

Hi! I'm Kinder. I was just sitting here thinking about how much fun I've been having in the garden. Have you ever eaten a tomato right off the vine or tasted a strawberry straight from the field? They are really yummy and taste way better than the ones from the store.

The best part is, no matter where you live, as long as you have dirt, you can grow fruits and veggies, even in the city. Want to know how? You do? Okay, I'm not just going to tell you, I'm going to show you!

My garden adventure actually started about a year ago when I was minding my own business skateboarding. All of a sudden my parents told me we were going for a little trip. Zoom, and off we went. We wound up going to a farm and boy was I in for a big surprise!

First of all, I had no idea that fruits and vegetables grew out of the ground. I just thought somehow they magically appeared at the grocery store for me to eat. Boy was I wrong! As soon as I got back to my home I created my own garden. Now, I don't live on a huge farm, but I've been able to grow my own fruits and vegetables. It's easy and a lot of fun.

The Basics

Basic #1: Here Comes the Sun

The Basics

All plants need four things:

1. Sun
2. Soil
3. Food
4. Water

I love the sun. It makes me feel good when it shines on me. Plants are the same way! They need sunshine to grow strong and green, especially fruits and vegetables. Most of them need 4 to 5 hours of direct sunlight every day.

No garden will grow without sunlight, so find a good, sunny place to put your garden. Look around your home to find a corner or spot that gets lots of sun (if it faces south, it will get the most sun), is easy to get water to, and isn't in someone else's way. You don't want to pick a spot where your brother will stomp all over it every afternoon during his football practice!

Try to find an area that does not get too much wind, though. Wind is not the vegetable gardener's friend. It makes leaves dry out and turn brown. Wind hurts the plants, and you will have to water more often.

Make a Sun Chart

This is a fun and easy way to choose the best place to start your garden.

Start with a plain sheet of paper and mark where your house is, as well as other things like patios, doghouses, and fences that can't be moved. Be sure to add in any big trees that shade an entire area. Then draw where you want to plant your garden. Once you have your drawing, watch the sun at different times of the day and mark with different colors which areas get direct sunlight. If the sun shines in the same area all day, you'll have several different colors in that area. More colors in an area means a better place to put your garden.

Basic #2: Getting Dirt-y.

Soil is just a fancy word for dirt, and it's my favorite part of gardening. If you're anything like me, you think playing in the dirt is a lot of fun. Well, guess what! I got really dirty gardening, and I didn't even get in trouble!

Not only is soil a lot of fun to play with, it's really important to plants. Plants grow their roots into the soil where they get water and food that they eat.

Make Mud Pies & Test Your Soil

Good soil will let water run through it, but not too fast. If the water flows too fast, it will take all the food away from the plants, but if the soil is too sticky, the water won't flow enough and the roots will drown.

The easiest way to figure out what kind of soil you have is to make mud pies. Who doesn't like making mud pies? Dig down six inches and get a clump of soil. Squeeze it tight in your hand and then open it. If the soil falls apart right away, it is sand. If the soil holds together but falls apart when you touch it, it is called silt or loam. If the soil stays together no matter what you do to it, it is clay.

Ideally, your soil would be a perfect mix of all three. However, since it is extremely rare to have perfect soil, it is best to add bagged soil to your garden whenever you plant anything. Your plants will thank you tons, I promise!

Basic #3: Food

I've heard of compost before, but I just thought it was a pile of trash. Well, I've learned that's not really true. A compost pile can include lots of things, such as leaves and grass clippings; shredded newspapers; and even kitchen scraps like potato peelings and eggshells.

If you're going to make your own compost pile, the key thing to remember is that it must be kept moist, but not soaked. Plants can only absorb the compost after it decomposes, and moisture is important for decomposition to happen. However, too much water can cause mold and mildew, which make it stink really bad. Peew!

Vegetables take a lot of food and nutrients out of soil compared to other kinds of plants. To get big and healthy crops, you'll need to put this food back into the soil so your veggies can keep eating. You can do this in three ways.

- Manure, which is really animal poop. I know this sounds pretty yucky to eat, but plants really like it!
- Compost, which is dead plants. They have lots of nutrients your plants can use, and you can find them in other areas of your garden, or even your kitchen.
- Fertilizer, which is usually made from dead plants or animals (organic fertilizer), or from special chemicals in a lab (inorganic).

Making Compost

To make a compost pile, all you need is a small area in your yard or even a small container. Then gather the right materials. Start by adding dry leaves or branches. Then add a couple of scoops of garden soil and top it off with things from the kitchen. Anything that rots will work, the more gross, the better. You can also visit a local coffee house and ask them to save their old coffee grounds for you to add to your pile. The coffee grounds can stop unwanted plants from growing in your compost pile, and they attract an extra bonus – earthworms!

Activity: Feed Your Plants

You can either dig the food into the soil as you're planting your veggies, or just spread it on top of the soil.

How Soil Is Remediated

If you have bad soil in your garden area, don't spend too much time trying to fix it. Instead, work on top of it by adding a raised garden bed. The good soil and roots from your plants will eventually dig into the bad soil and enrich it as well.

Basic #4: Water

Good sun, soil, and food are really important, but no plants can grow without water. Just like people need water to grow big and strong, so do plants. When you first plant your garden, the crops will need more water to get started. Too little water can wilt your plants and they'll turn yellow and die, but too much water can make your plants drown. If you're lucky, you'll get just the right amount of rain to help your plants grow, but you've got to give lots of attention to your garden to make sure it's getting the right amount of water.

One thing you can do to reduce the amount of water needed in your garden is to add mulch. Mulch helps keep moisture in the ground. You can use grass clippings, newspapers with leaves, straw, or bagged mulch made from cedar or other wood chips.

Mulch fights off weeds too. It's kind of like the super hero of the garden!

Working with Fresh Seeds

Vegetables are actually some of the easiest plants to grow, and I think when you grow them from seeds, it's even more rewarding. When I first saw my first sprout from a seed, I couldn't stop smiling. However, if you're taking fresh seeds straight out of veggies, be aware that they may be stubborn seeds that never sprout, no matter how well you care for them. It can be a fun test, but don't get upset if the seeds don't bloom.

If you decide you want to use fresh seeds, here are a couple of things to help you out:

1. Try not to choose vegetables that have been processed with pesticides, hormones or additives.
2. Do not take the seeds out of the vegetables until they have had time to fully mature. Leave the vegetables out at room temperature until they start to look aged, meaning they start to wrinkle up and/or turn brown.
3. Pumpkin, squash, tomato, cucumber, and pepper seeds are covered with a squishy substance. It's good to let them sit out overnight in their surrounding gel. Then rinse the seeds and let them air dry for several days. Then store the seeds in small paper bags or envelopes in a cool place like a pantry until you're ready to plant them.
4. Prepare the soil and area like you would for any store bought seed and plant away.

See Your Seeds

Seeds come in all shapes and sizes and often don't really look anything like the plant or vegetable they're going to grow up to be. When you become an expert gardener you'll actually be able to look at a seed and know exactly what it's going to grow in to. Hard to imagine, huh? Well, you can start practicing your gardening skills now by matching the seeds on the left to the veggie they'll turn into on the right.

It's okay if you don't get any right at first, but after you finish this garden book you'll be able to ace the test!

Answers: 1. B - Carrot Seeds, 2. E – Cucumber Seeds, 3. A - Radish Seeds, 4. C- Tomato Seeds, 5. D – Watermelon Seeds.

Tools Fit for a Kid's Garden

It's a lot easier to work in the garden if you have tools and gloves that fit. Ever try to hold a grown up sized shovel? Did you feel like you were going to fall over? Ouch. When tools are too heavy, or too big to use the right way, I just get frustrated, and that's no fun. That's why it's so important to have the right gear. Here's a list of what I have to use in my garden:

A wheelbarrow makes moving things from place to place a lot easier.

My favorite tool in the garden is this kid sized sink. It makes filling up watering cans easy and fun. Plus, playing with water is almost as fun as playing in dirt. You can even do both! It's giggleicious!

Who doesn't love to dig in the dirt? A small spade or shovel is awesome for our little hands. I've tried plastic shovels, but they don't work for me. They're perfect for playing in the sand but can be easily broken in the thick and solid soil of the garden.

A watering can is a must-have in any garden...big or small. Plants need to be watered regularly, and a tyke-sized can makes giving plants a drink a lot easier.

Adult Helpers: Investing in high-quality tools will be worth it. You want the tools to survive the rough and tumble job of gardening with kids.

It's All in the Bag!

If you have only a small space to garden like a balcony or patio, have rock-filled soil, or just want to experiment like me, you can still be a super gardener! Try getting a few bags of potting soil and planting your veggies right in the bag!

1. Start by poking small holes in the side of each bag for drainage. If the extra water can't escape, the roots will sit in it and eventually rot.

2. Next, cut one large hole on top for the plants.

3. Plant your veggies. My friends and I chose three herbs to put in one bag: rosemary, parsley, and chives.

4. Cover the bag in mulch and presto, instant garden. You can now treat this bag just like any piece of land. Water it and watch your food grow.

The Magic Bean

Now that the idea of gardening and the basics have your attention lets start thinking about what you want to plant in your garden. A fun way to start coming up with ideas for your garden is to draw it.

Glue a lima bean or other bean onto a white piece of paper. From there draw what you would like to see in your garden.

This is a great project to use your imagination and get inspired for what you want to plant!

Section 2

Growing Vegetables

Not all vegetables grown in the garden are alike and they are grouped together depending on what part of the plant is eaten. There are actually eight groups of vegetables. Can you name them. What part of the vegetable do you eat?

Varieties of Vegetables

BULB (Onion, Garlic)

FRUIT (Tomato, Pepper)

TUBER (Potato, Yam)

STEM (Celery, Asparagus)

ROOT (Radish, Carrot, Beet)

SEED (Corn, Bean)

LEAF (Lettuce, Cabbage)

FLOWER BUD (Broccoli, Artichoke)

The Carrot Patch

I like to grow carrots simply because I love to eat them. Carrots are yummy from the store, but they taste even better when they're fresh from the garden. I got so excited the first time I grew a carrot that I didn't even wash the dirt off before taking a big bite. Take it from me, wash the dirt first THEN eat the carrot. It tastes a whole lot better.

Besides tasting good, carrots are packed with nutrients. The thing that makes them bright orange is called carotene, which changes to vitamin A when you eat it. My doctor says that Vitamin A helps me see better, especially at night.

Carrots are ideal for the garden because they grow easily from seeds and are a great way to see plant grow from seed to vegetable.

Carrots grow best in raised garden beds that get a lot of sunlight. A raised garden bed is a garden built on top of the ground. They can either be contained with a wood frame or simply be a mound of dirt piled high.

The carrot is actually the root of the carrot plant, so the deeper your garden is, the more room the carrot will have to grow. Be sure to read the seed pack to see when it's best to start planting carrots in your area.

Caring for Carrots

When the carrots start to pop up, you may need to thin them out a bit by pulling out some small ones that look like they're too close together. Carrots should have at least two to three inches between them when they are growing.

Weeds and carrots don't go well together, so you should check your carrots each day and pull out anything that looks like a yucky weed.

Once you have your raised bed, make a shallow groove or small ditch down the center of the bed.

The groove should be about a 1/2 inch deep or maybe one small pinkie finger.

Tip: Mix the seeds with a handful of sand so that the seedlings don't get too overcrowded and sprinkle seeds along the row.

Cover the seeds lightly and water. You want the soil to be moist but not flooded.

Adult Helpers: Before your kids eat their carrots, help them measure them or trace them into a carrot log book. It's a great way for them to keep count of how many carrots they've grown, and it's really fun to see just how big they can grow a carrot. Maybe they can even draw their carrots into carrot people and make a story about the veggies they've grown.

Radical Radishes

Growing radishes is fast and easy. It's actually the first vegetable that popped up in my first garden, and I have to tell you I couldn't help smiling.

Just drop the seeds into a row about two inches apart from each other, lightly cover them with soil, and wait for them to come up!

As a root vegetable, radishes grow underground so you won't be able to see them grow like corn or tomatoes. In just about three weeks you should start to see the tiny red radish starting to peak out. Once they have matured, they are super fun to pluck out of the ground.

Adult Helpers: Keep in mind that radishes are fun to grow but not as much fun for kids to eat. The sharp taste can be offensive. Your child will be proud of the contribution to the family so try to disguise the odd taste by mixing small pieces of it into a vegetable stir-fry, salad, or even a chicken salad sandwich.

Corn

Get an earful!

Corn is everywhere!

If you're anything like me you've probably had cornflakes for breakfast. Have you ever had a piece of cornbread with dinner? What about a piece of corn on the cob with melted butter? I'm sure you've been treated to popcorn at the movies?

Corn is one of the world's major crops and is used to make all those yummy foods above. Corn is a seed vegetable that has a hairy green layer called a husk surrounding the yellow kernels.

Corn is a delicious vegetable that tastes even better when you pick it and rush it straight to the stovetop. That's because its sugar turns to starch in the blink of an eye. If you store the corn too long you will not get to taste the sugars, so the fresher the better.

Where to Grow

Corn needs full sun, and lots of nice warm soil. For these two reasons, the ideal spot is against a wall, in an area that gets six or more hours of clear sunlight daily. Walls can reflect additional sunlight onto the corn, and what light is not reflected gets absorbed into the soil, changes to heat, and is released to keep the corn warm at night.

However, even the smallest garden can produce some golden ears of corn. Growing corn doesn't have to just take place in large cornfields. You can even grow your own corn in a small pot or container.

Adult Helpers: It's cool to be corny, but it can take corn up to 90 days to mature, so you'll want to continue to make it interesting once the new wears off. Following are a couple of ideas:

Did You Know that... an average ear of corn has 800 kernels and 16 rows?

Corncob Painting

No brushes needed... just a few ears of corn, paint, and a canvas to paint on.

Dip the corncobs in paint and roll them along large sheets of paper. You can try comparing paintings made with cobs with kernels to those made with cobs without kernels. Silks can add interesting textures, and husks can even be used as the canvas in place of paper.

Corny Race

Why not stage a race, especially if you have more than one young gardener? Let each one plant their own corn, then watch to see who grows the tallest stalk or pops out a piece of corn first. To make the contest fair, each child should be responsible for watering, weeding, and caring for their own plants.

Lettuce Play

Did You Know that... lettuce is the only vegetable that is never frozen, canned, dried, cooked, processed or sold in any way but fresh?

When I was first deciding to grow lettuce in my garden, I asked my mom to take me to the grocery store, and I was surprised to find out that there are lots of different kinds.

What's your favorite? Mine's the one that's shaped like a small soccer ball with tight wrinkly leaves.

It's called Iceberg lettuce. But there's also butterhead lettuce, which just sounds funny. Romaine tastes good on a turkey sandwich. There are so many to choose from.

Want to know why I really like lettuce? In some places lettuce grows so fast it can go from seed to salad plate in just a little over three weeks. Now that's super speed gardening.

The ideal place to grow any type of lettuce is in loose, well-drained soil in a partially sunny garden spot. It's mostly water, so if it gets too much sun, it will dry out and burn. Lettuce likes cool air and lots of moisture, so if you live in a hot place, find an area with some shade or plant the lettuce in the shade of tomato or cucumber plants. Plenty of water and a healthy dose of fertilizer will get it growing fast.

Sow, or place, the lettuce seeds in rows, following the directions on the seed packet you've chosen.

Pick lettuce as soon as they look like they are ready to use. It is really fun to pretend you are a rabbit hopping along. As pretend rabbits, when you see leaves ready to eat, hop over and "nibble" or pluck off the outer leaves. Leaf lettuces will grow back after cutting, which is really cool because you do not have to reseed it.

For butterhead lettuce or iceberg, cut the entire plant at ground level.

Adult Helpers: Kids will take great pride in growing their own plants, and before you know it, they'll be in the kitchen making a fresh salad to eat.

Kinder Kitchen Corner: Tear off and wash large lettuce leaves. Place a spoonful of chicken or tuna salad in the middle of each one. Roll up and chill. These are great for school lunches or a midday snack.

Totally Tomatoes

Hands-down, tomatoes rule in any vegetable garden. Seriously, what would pasta, pizza, and ketchup be without tomatoes?

The color and shape vary a lot depending on the variety you choose to grow. Some are egg-shaped, some are the size of a ping pong ball, and some are even heart-shaped. "Celebrity," "Beefsteak," and "cherry" tomatoes are great varieties to try for first-time tomato growers because they taste great right off the vine.

Tomatoes prefer a warm dry climate and, like most other plants, grow best in well-drained soils. Remember, well drained soil means it is not hard clay, but loose enough that you could easily stick a shovel in it to dig a hole. Tomatoes love the sun, and the more you can give them, the better they'll grow.

Tomatoes are great for any kid garden because they are easy to grow in containers. They can grow in patio pots, window boxes, or even hanging baskets. Just make sure they have room to spread out. Also, since tomato plants grow upward rather than outward, it is important to give the plant some extra support to keep the weight of the tomato from pulling the plant to the ground. The best way to do this is to use stakes, cages, or trellises.

Tomatoes grow best in the summer months when the temperatures are above 75 degrees. When the temperatures get above 90 degrees, give your plants a little bit more attention. They may even need to be watered twice a day. Tomatoes can grow in colder weather but may not taste as good. If you live where it gets extra cold, like where it even snows, try growing your tomatoes in a greenhouse.

Tomatoes are ready to pick when they have turned red, like the color of my shirt, and are just slightly soft when you squeeze them.

Tomatoes are great container plants.

Start seedlings indoors, or buy them at your local nursery.

Tomato vines need support when they start bearing fruit. You'll want to have a wire cage or trellis for them.

Warning: Avoid over watering tomatoes. Cut back on watering when the tomato has reached full size. Otherwise, the skin is likely to burst and explode like a water balloon. Yeah, it sounds kind of cool, but it definitely makes a mess, and if the tomato explodes you can't eat it.

Really Cool Project!

If you really want to impress your friends with your green thumb, grow tomatoes in a bottle. "Impossible bottles" are bottles with things inside that are too big to have been put through the neck of the bottle, like a ship.

Begin when a tomato is small enough to go through the bottle's neck. Use a plastic bottle that is light enough to tie to the plant without damaging it, but big enough to hold a ripe tomato. A plastic drink bottle will work great.

Find a tomato small enough to push through the bottle's neck, and with a long stem. Tie the bottle to the branch using twist ties or string. Be careful not to tie the bottle on too tight. Just enough so it will stay in place.

The bottle will act like a mini-greenhouse, holding moisture and heat inside. This will help the tomato ripen faster. If it gets too hot, though, the tomato might get scorched, so if you have a little shade try placing your bottled plant there.

Once the tomato is fully ripe, cut the stem and untie the bottle. Now amaze your friends with your "impossible bottle."

Tomatoes in a bag!

You can easily grow tomatoes straight from potting soil bags too. The secret to success here is to stack two bags on top of each other.

1. Tomatoes like to have deep roots, so doubling up the bags will give your plants the room they need to grow healthy fruit.

2. After you poke holes in the side for drainage, cut a hole on the top of the bottom bag and bottom of the top bag. Then stack them. You've just made a bigger planter! Don't worry if there is a little space between the bags because a little extra drainage is good.

3. Next, cut one hole on top and place your tomato plant. You should have one plant per stack to give it enough space for the roots to spread out as they grow.

4. Press the soil gently around the plant, and you are set to go. For best results, place the bags where the tomato plant gets at least seven hours of sunlight each day.

Cucumber Madness

Ever hear the saying, "cool as a cucumber?" Well, cucumbers are totally cool to watch grow. They're torpedo shaped and usually a dark green color. Cucumbers are 95 percent water, so if you're ever going to the desert, take them with you!

Cucumbers do like to sprawl, or spread out, while they're growing. They have the same growing patterns as squash and zucchini. If you don't have a lot of room, plant cucumbers next to a fence or trellis. You can train them to grow up instead of out.

If your cucumbers taste bitter, it is probably because they are not getting enough water. For some reason, cucumbers seem to need more water than the rest of the garden. My friend Michael gave me a great suggestion for making sure my cucumbers don't get too thirsty. Turn the page and we'll show you how.

Take a one-gallon jug or can and have an adult helper make holes all around the bottom. Then, bury it in the ground next to your cucumber plant.

Use the garden hose to fill the container with water several times a week. The water will slowly drip throughout the day to water the cucumbers when they need it.

Kinder Kitchen Corner: After you've picked your cucumbers, take a slice and make a cut halfway down the middle. Hang the slice on a big glass of lemonade. The crunchiness goes great with the refreshing drink.

Green Bean Hideout!

Need a place to get away from it all? Or maybe just a healthy hideout? Try creating a fun foliage teepee. It's easy. Plus, every beginner vegetable garden should include green beans. The seeds are big, sturdy, and really easy to handle. Turn the page and we'll show you how.

Here's what you need; long stakes or bamboo poles, packets of pole bean seeds, string, and room to build.

1. Prepare an area, about six square feet, with good soil. Use supplemental soil if needed.

2. Make a teepee shape with stakes or bamboo poles.

3. Use string to tie the stake tops together and then push the ends of the poles into the ground.

4. Tie string between each pole so the vines will have something to attach to. Don't forget to leave one side open so you can hide inside!

5. Soak the bean seeds overnight to give them a head start and soften the exterior coating so they can sprout quicker. Plant four or five seeds at the base of each pole. Cover them with about an inch of dirt.

6. Water the seeds and growing vines frequently, about an inch of water a week. Also, avoid getting the leaves wet to keep the plant from getting sick or diseased.

7. Once you see a second set of leaves grow, it's time to mulch. The mulch will help keep the moisture in the soil.

8. Wait for the vines to grow, and in about six to eight weeks, you'll have the perfect edible hideout. It's really fun to snack on a bean or two while you are in there.

9. Why stop with a teepee? Try building an entire castle next time!

Kinder Kitchen Corner: Green beans are full of fiber, protein, B-vitamins, beta carotene, calcium, and potassium. The beans can be eaten fresh or harvested and cooked. Try roasting green beans for a tasty treat. Lightly coat about twenty beans on a baking sheet with 2 tbsp of extra-virgin olive oil. Salt and pepper to taste. Roast at 400 degrees Fahrenheit for approximately 25 minutes. Serve at room temperature and watch your kids become green bean junkies!

Sunny Sunflowers

Harvesting Tip: When the back of the flower head starts to turn brown it's time to harvest. Cut off the blossom that holds all the seeds, keeping a small piece of the stalk attached. Cover the head with a small bag or piece of fabric. Tie a ribbon to the stem to keep the bag secure to catch the seeds and hang the covered flower upside down. As the flower dries, the seeds will fall into the bag and be perfect for eating or replanting.

Vibrant and cheery, sunflowers are easy to grow from just a seed. They are also one of the fastest growing plants in the garden. It used to be that sunflowers only grew on a farm, but you can grow them almost anywhere! They can grow in the corner of a yard, or even in a large pot.

Be sure to find an area for your sunflowers that is in full sun and has enough room for the plant to grow to its maximum size. If you're planting in a pot or small container, try the "Teddy Bear" variety. I really love the "fuzzy" look and it grows to only about 18 inches tall. If you want to go way huge look for "Russian Giants" or "Kong" sunflowers. They can grow as tall as 15 feet, so you'll need plenty of space, but they are worth it!

When planting sunflowers find a place that gets full sun. Seeds or plants should be about six inches apart. Then, like all the other plants in your garden, water.

Did You Know...

Most people think we call them sunflowers because they look like flower suns, but that's not really how they got their name. The real reason is because sunflowers will turn their head from east to west everyday following the sun. Pretty cool, huh?

Section 3

The Fun Stuff

Pizza Garden

Grow your own toppings!

Did you know you could grow a pizza right in your garden? Okay, so you can't really grow a pizza, but you can grow the yummy toppings. A really cool way to do this is to make your garden actually look like a pizza.

All you have to do is use an old wagon wheel to give the pizza garden its shape. In each hole, or "slice," you can grow a different vegetable to put on your pizza.

1. Begin by clearing out an area for growing a bunch of different types of vegetables. Look for a spot that gets at least four hours of sun a day.

2. Place an old wagon wheel firmly in the dirt. If you don't have a wheel don't worry. You can use rocks, bricks, or cedar mulch to outline a circle.

3. Fill the slices with good soil for the best crops.

4. Fill each slice with vegetables and herbs that make great pizza toppings.

There are a gazillion things you could grow in your pizza garden. Tomatoes, bell peppers, basil, oregano, onions, rosemary, spinach, zucchini, and even corn are some of my favorites.

Roma tomatoes are good in a pizza garden because they're small, grow fast, and have a thick meaty skin, which add texture to your pizza.

Oregano is a perennial herb, which means you can keep getting more oregano from the same plant year after year. Oregano gives pizza a wonderful smell.

Yellow squash is colorful, and when you slice it really thin, it cooks perfectly on a pizza.

My taste buds always get excited by basil, so I think you should add in one or two basil plants to every pizza garden. Sweet basil is the yummiest!

Even though there's no such thing as a pepperoni shrub yet, I promise you'll enjoy your homegrown pizza.

Covering the area with a layer of mulch will help keep the weeds out.

Chives are one of the easiest plants to grow. In about a week you'll start to see something, and you can eat every part of the plant.

Adult Helpers: Kids and pizza go together like macaroni and cheese. A homegrown pizza garden is a special way to build memories with your children. When the vegetables are ready, encourage your young gardeners to invite their friends over for a pizza party. Allow guests to create custom pizzas using miniature pre-baked pizza crusts and offer the fresh toppings in bowls. When pizzas are piled high with toppings grown by your kids, it will become a memorable childhood moment of pride and self worth. This is a great way to encourage getting the vegetables from the plant to plate.

Window Box

There are a loads and loads of ideas for planting a garden, even when you don't think you have enough space for one. If you have a window, you have a place for a garden by planting a window box.

A window box is a small container that, believe it or not, can be planted with just about anything. They are usually mounted under a window or placed on a windowsill.

Window boxes come in all kinds of shapes and sizes. There are really expensive and fancy ones, and there are simple and cheap ones. Fortunately, plants aren't too picky and will love anything you pick as long as there are holes for drainage.

Once you decide on which type of window box you want, prepare the box for planting. First, adult helpers should securely install the brackets or anchors for the window box. Remember, once it is filled with soil and water it will weigh quite a bit more.

1. Choose your plants. Mixing three or more herbs together looks really nice because of the different shades of green. One of my favorites to grow in a window box is basil because it grows well in shallow soil. Rosemary is another herb you should think about putting in your window box because pests will stay away from it, and it can do well even when it's not watered enough.

2. Then it's time to plant your window box. Do this the same way you would plant any garden pot or container. To keep things simple and to keep your soil pure and weed free, use a bag of ready to plant bagged potting soil. If you're planting "starter" herbs, plants that already have leaves, they should be spaced about 3 or 4 inches apart and within 1/2 inch of the surface of the soil.

3. As you place the starter plants into the soil, break up the roots gently just in case the roots are all tied together. Roots want to be free to grow. Be gentle so you don't break them, but separate them so they don't fight each other to grow.

4. Now it's time to grab your adult helper, hang the window box in place, and enjoy the fruits, or more appropriately, the "herbs," of your labor. Water your plants frequently but don't soak them. When the soil starts to feel dry, it is time to water again! If the soil sticks to your fingers in clumps, it has enough water already.

Taste Test Activity

Now that you've become an expert gardener and have even learned about the most outrageous veggies, it's time to train your taste buds. First, stick out your tongue and get them warmed up! (Giggling also can warm up your taste buds.) Now, have an adult helper cut and cook a number of vegetables from your garden. Then put on a blindfold and try the different vegetables. See if you can guess what they are. You might even taste a vegetable you didn't know you liked. This can also be a fun game to do with a group of friends.

Creative Container Gardening

Sometimes the smallest of areas can get a little extra pizzazz with a creative container garden. You can grow things in just about anything. Flower pots work fine, but don't be stopped if you don't have any. If it can hold dirt, chances are it'll work. From a cup to a bucket, or even an old toy, anything goes.

I came up with some creative containers that are easy to plant in. Make sure you get something that can get wet. If it has holes in it that's even better.

Colander Herb Garden

Kitchen colanders provide a good amount of space to begin growing a handy little herb garden. You could also plant lettuce in a container like this. The holes of the colander were made for drainage, so it is really easy to plant because, as we've learned, plants need well-drained soil. And regardless of the weather, a colander with herbs can be at your fingertips year round because you can place it inside or outside.

1. Add pea gravel or small stones in the bottom to help with drainage.
2. Add in a handful or two of soil. Fill the colander up to the top of the holes.
3. Add in your favorite herbs. Shown here are basil and parsley.
4. Then water and check your colander herb garden everyday to see your herbs growth.

Rain Boot Planter

Are your rain boots too small to go puddle jumping? Don't throw them away! Instead try using an old pair as a pot for your plants. They're obviously rugged enough for the outdoors and cute enough to create a bunch of giggles.

Cucumbers or melons are a good choice to plant because they will cascade or hang over the sides and look really neat.

We were really proud of this one, so we put them where our friends and neighbors could see them...smack in the middle of the front yard. They're great because we can even move them as they grow!

1. Grab an adult to help you drill a couple of holes about 1/2 inch wide in the bottom and side of each boot for drainage.

2. Add small rocks or gravel until half of the boot is full.

3. Add in soil or planting mix, enough to fill the boot about an inch from the top, while still leaving room for your plants.

Recycled Toy Wagon and Ball Planters

Unlike ordinary gardens where your plants are rooted in one place, container gardens allow you to take your garden with you to show off to your friends and classmates. And you know what's really fun to use as a container? I like recycling some of my old toys. Just imagine your friends' surprise when you bounce in with a pepper growing inside a playground ball or have squash coming out of an old wagon.

1. Pick out a colorful toy or wagon.
2. Have an adult helper poke a few holes in the bottom with a nail and hammer for drainage.
3. Fill the bottom of the toy with 1 to 2 inches of pea gravel.
4. Fill the toy about half-way up with potting soil.
5. Carefully remove the starter plants from their containerc and break up their roots. Then place them inside the toy and add more soil until the roots are all covered.
6. Water the newly planted garden, and that's it! You can put the garden in a place of honor, take it with you to it show off, or even move it around so it can get the right amount of sun.

Water Tip: Don't forget to poke your finger gently into the soil. If it feels dry about an inch below the surface, it's time to water. Of course, if the plant looks sad or is wilting, that's a great signal to water it too.

Hang This!

A Hanging Vegetable Planter

Don't let small spaces frustrate you. Even in the most cramped places, you can enjoy your own fruits and vegetables by creating a hanging garden out of a wire frame basket. It's ideal for a small space like a balcony or porch because it grows up instead of out. Hanging wire baskets are easy to find at garden shops.

1. Place one of the baskets on top of a bucket or large pot for an easier place to work. Take a handful or two of peat moss or sphagnum moss and line the bottom of each basket about a quarter of the way up. Peat moss comes from a family of wild growing mosses and will help fertilize the plants as well as create a bottom to the basket so the soil doesn't fall out.

2. Scoop potting soil into the bottom of the basket. Add moss and soil in layers as you work your way up the side of the basket. It was helpful to have four hands to make these stacked baskets.

3. Water the baskets really thoroughly and leave it on the bucket to drain for about an hour. Then hang it in a place that gets at least a couple of hours of sunlight a day, and you should be able to reach it for easy watering.

4. We used basil, oregano, and parsley for making spaghetti sauce in this basket. Plants that like to hang, like strawberries and rosemary, would be perfect to use too. Use enough plants to cover the entire basket, but leave enough space for them to grow.

Depending on what you chose to plant, you should be able to start eating from the basket in a matter of weeks. So what are you waiting for?

Umbrella "Root" Garden

I've had a lot of fun imagining how I could recycle old junk into planters. My favorite is this old plastic umbrella because you can actually watch the roots grow! I was amazed to see the plants grow two ways – not only up out of the soil, but down into the ground as well. This is beyond neato!

1. Here's what you need: a clear umbrella, potting soil, pea gravel, and your plants. You could use things like squash or beans, but I thought it would be cool to grow fresh toppings for an ice cream sundae! Raspberries, strawberries, and chocolate mint are an excellent dessert mix.

2. Remember all plants need the soil to drain in order to get a good balanced supply of water and nutrients, so an adult should use a small nail to puncture the umbrella and create drainage holes.

3. Place the umbrella where you want your garden, then add a small amount of pea gravel inside. This helps with drainage, and will help the umbrella stand upside down.

4. Next fill up half the umbrella with soil.

5. Start planting. I used gardener's tape to tie the raspberry vine to the umbrella handle to train it to grow up rather than out.

Adult Helpers: You'll get visible roots in just a matter of days, so your young gardeners will see the roots while the work is still fresh in their memory. Mint is ideal for this project because the roots are invasive, meaning once the roots start to grow they may not stop. However, their invasive roots may choke out other plants.

Growing a root view garden is a great science-fair project. If the umbrella is too big, try using a milk carton and clear piece of hard plastic or acrylic from a hardware store. Plant your seeds at least eight weeks ahead of time so the roots can really take off.

Out of This World Veggies

Now that you know how to garden, try to grow something that will surprise your friends. These vegetables may even creep them out a bit because they are so crazy!

I think these are the coolest of the cool vegetables!

Squash. It's a verb. It's a sport. But what I really care about is that it's also a vegetable... a funny looking vegetable too! Squash are great to have in the garden because they grow fast and can get really big. Grown straight on the vine, they look like bells. Take pictures of the squash each week and see how much it changes.

My favorite color is blue, so when I grew these blue potatoes I could not have been more excited. Digging for these blue nuggets is like digging for buried treasures. Once you find them, the 'All Blue' potatoes are delicious, mashed or stuffed!

Carrots are the great surprise of the garden. You never know what you're going to get until you pull it out of the ground. Imagine pulling out a purple carrot! These carrots, called 'purple haze,' are definitely the talk of the garden. Surprisingly, they still have a bright orange center when you cut them up for a snack.

If you like aliens, you'll probably love growing 'Egyptian Walking' onions. They look like something crazy that just landed from outer space. Unlike other onions that grow in the ground, these grow like a small tree with the onion bulb on top of the stem. They do have a strong taste, so you only need a small amount when flavoring your food with them.

My favorite green beans aren't even green. I know, it's crazy but true. They're purple, and they look like grape juice! They're called 'Royal Burgundy' and are a great attention getter in the garden. The purple beans are really fun to pick because they're easy to spot in the green leaves. When you cook these beans they play a fun trick. The purple beans turn green.

Photos of All Blue potatoes, Purple Haze carrots, Egyptian Walking onions, Royal Burgundy beans and Chiogga beets are courtesy of Territorial Seed Company.

I thought beets were Yucky with a capital Y! They're almost as bad as brussel sprouts. Well, that was until I grew a Chiogga beet. Chiogga beets are just cool! When sliced, they look a lot like a candy cane with rings of red and white. Better yet, the two-inch balls have a sweet tasty flavor.

Making Garden Markers

Creative and Crafty Garden Markers

As you plant your garden, especially if you're using any of the outrageous veggies on page 57, you should add a few markers to help you remember what is planted where. Nurseries and other specialty stores sell garden markers, but you can also make your own with items you can find lying around your house.

I made my garden markers out of thick tree branches, glass aquarium pebbles, and even rocks.

For Adult Helpers: Making garden markers is a great way to keep garden interest growing during the winter months. You can plan what you want to grow when the weather warms up and create these markers ahead of time.

For the tree branch markers, if you can't find a piece of wood the right size, ask an adult helper to cut a thick branch for you. Then paint one side. I used white primer paint, but you can use anything you have around the house. Once it dries, grab some permanent markers and draw pictures of the vegetables you're going to grow. Then ask an adult helper to drill a small hole in the bottom and insert a wood dowel, twig, or even a pencil in it to use as a stake.

Rocks can also be great garden markers. Use permanent markers to draw vegetables or names on them of what's going to grow in your garden. An adult helper can use an old coat hanger to create a stake for it and attach it with hot glue.

For the glass pebble markers, start by drawing vegetables on a very small piece of paper. It shouldn't be any larger than the pebbles you're using. Then use rubber cement to glue the paper in between two glass pebbles and wait for it to dry. Next, ask an adult helper to attach the glass pebbles to a twig with hot glue. After it dries, seal the cracks with more rubber cement to help protect it from water. If you want you can add a little raffia ribbon and they're ready to plant in your garden.

Glossary

If you came across a word you did not quite understand, you turned to the right page. All the words listed here were new to me, so I thought I would pass on their meanings to you.

Acrylic – a quick drying clear blob that hardens into a plastic like sheet.

Bud – an undeveloped part of the plant. May be a leaf, flower, or shoot for a new plant.

Bulb – an underground stem usually surrounded by leaves that are filled with food to help the plant grow; such as an onion.

Carotene – an orange-yellow to red pigment in plants which converts to vitamin A when eaten.

Compost – a mixture of degraded matter, like leaves or manure, used to improve soil and provide nutrients to plants.

Fahrenheit – a temperature scale that marks the freezing point of water at 32 degrees and the boiling point at 212 degrees.

Fertilizer – a food, including compost and manure, spread on or worked into the soil to help plants grow.

Flower – the reproductive structure of some seed-bearing plants.

Greenhouse – a structure, usually made of glass, where temperature and humidity can be controlled for growing young plants.

Husk – a thin dry covering of a seed or fruit; like on an ear of corn.

Kernel – a grain or seed enclosed in a husk.

Kinder – your new best friend. In German, my name means children.

Manure – animal poop, or dung, that is used to fertilize, or feed, plants.

Moisture – wetness that can be felt as vapor in the air. Dampness.

Mulch – a covering such as straw or leaves spread on the ground to help with water loss or stop weeds.

Nutrient – a source of nourishment.

Pea gravel – small round rock, less than 1/2 inch round.

Perennial – a plant that lives for more than two seasons and does not die after flowering or bearing fruit.

Pod – a long narrow seedcase containing peas, beans, etc.

Recycle – to re-use things.

Root – the underground part of a plant used for feeding the plant and holding the plant in place.

Sow – to plant seeds by throwing them.

Stem – a slender stalk or trunk supporting or connecting another plant part, such as a leaf or flower.

Trellis – a frame of lattice work to grow climbing plants on.

Tuber – an underground clump of stems with one bud at the bottom, such as a potato.

Resources

Custom Made Wagons
West Coast Wagons
(818) 355-5571
www.westcoastwagons.com
info@westcoastwagons.com

Durable Outdoor Toys & Products
Step 2
(866) 429-5200
www.step2.com

Family Farms
Tapia Brothers Farms
5251 Hayvenhurst Avenue
Encino, CA 91316
(818) 905-6155

Underwood Family Farms
3370 Sunset Valley Road
Moorpark, CA 93021
(805) 529-3690
www.underwoodfamilyfarms.com

Garden Products
Homeplace Structures
(866) 768-8465
www.homeplacestructures.com

Kellogg Garden Products
www.kellogggarden.com

Monrovia Nursery
www.monrovia.com

Stover Seed Company
(800) 621-0315
www.stoverseed.com

Acknowledgments

We would like to thank all of the children and families who were enthusiastic about working on all our various projects and willing to let us take their picture along the way. Our thanks to the family of Tapia Farms, who not only shared their land with us, but shared their knowledge. Sincere thanks to Monrovia Nursery for your continued support.

Thank you to Jennifer Kelley Lublin. Your photography is beautiful and amazing. Working with you has been a blast.

Thank you to Kelsey Ward. Your illustrations are full of energy. You are so talented, and we look forward to seeing where your art takes you. Huge high-five to Rachel Shachar for helping to bring Kinder to life.

We also need to give a special thank you to Ryan for putting up with us and your generous help in keeping us in line and on track. To Carla, for your constant hard work and scheduling. Elaine, your help, friendship, and support has made this process not only easier, but a lot of fun. And kudos to Robin for your hospitality and generosity.

About the Authors

Lisa Ely is an award-winning television and documentary producer. With over fifteen years of experience in producing shows for networks like HGTV, TLC, and Discovery, Lisa has become an expert in home design and gardening.

It was on Discovery Home's "Garden Police" where she first met and worked with Michael.

Lisa also has been a volunteer director at Camp Good Times for children with cancer for more than fifteen years. During that time, she has helped create and implement outdoor programs for campers of all ages.

Lisa received her degree in Broadcast Journalism from the University of Southern Californa. She received an MBA from Pepperdine University and studied International Business and Marketing at Oxford University and the University of Antwerp. Lisa currently lives in Southern California with her husband and two children. She writes:

"I first discovered the idea of growing my own vegetables when I was quite young. I remember as soon as my mother introduced me to the snails and lizards in the muddy garden, I was hooked. I loved pulling up the radishes, cutting the lettuce, and walking through tunnels of green beans looking for the longest ones I could find. To this day, the sound of snapping crisp beans takes me back to those happy days in the garden.

"I was about five when I first asked my dad for a patch in the yard to grow vegetables myself. I remember the first seeds I sowed, and how proud I was to serve the carrots I had grown all by myself. Now my enthusiasm for growing vegetables has rubbed off on my own family, and deciding which vegetables to plant and eat has become a family activity we all enjoy.

"I've learned from my own children, ages three and one, that creating gardens for children means involving the kids in every part of the garden. If you let them design, plant, water, and harvest the garden, you'll be amazed at what their little green thumbs can do!

"Get gardening!"

Michael Glassman is an award winning landscape designer and owner of one of Northern California's most prestigious design firms. He has more than thirty years of experience in creating outdoor living environments and was co-host and designer for Discovery Home Channel's series "Garden Police" for two years. Part environmental evangelist, part landscape design coach and connoisseur, Michael regularly appears as a guest on a number of television shows on networks like HGTV and Discovery.

He has authored several books on landscaping, including *Outdoor Designs for Living*.

Michael received his degree in Landscape Design and Horticulture from the University of California at Davis and studied at LaNapoule Art Foundation in France. His work can be viewed at www.michaelglassman.com. He writes:

"I am the original Kinder! I was raised in the city, and I probably was as naive as most and believed vegetables were grown in the grocery store. Until recently, I never had my own vegetable garden. Yes, I am a landscape designer who creates beautiful outdoor environments and understands the biology of plants, but growing my own fruits and vegetables never entered into my world.

"Kinder's exploration into vegetable gardening reflects my own learning about growing fruits and vegetables. This year I planted my second vegetable garden. The melons are ripening, and the bounty is amazing. My satisfaction is unbelievable.

"Like Kinder and a number of kids I know, there are plenty of vegetables I cannot stomach. So, we really tried to focus on vegetables that Kinder and kids found to be their favorites.

"Think of what gardening for food can do for you and your family. Enjoy your journey!"

About the Photographer

Jennifer Kelley Lublin is a professional photographer living in Southern California who specializes in working with children. Her mission is to inspire by shining a light on people through art.

You can visit her website at www.JKLphotos.com.

About Kinder

Kinder is a little boy who thirsts to understand everything around him. It's not enough for him to know that something simply works, or happens, or even IS. He needs to understand how and why. He is curious to no end, and loves to explore new things with his family and friends. Kinder is often described as being hyper, but that's probably just because he giggles a lot.

When he doesn't know something, Kinder actually enjoys it because it gives him the opportunity to learn and find out something new. Learning is an adventure, and he will always share what he learns with others.

Kinder is committed to helping you smile. His goals are to foster within each of his friends a positive self-esteem, confidence, caring for our planet, having fun together as a family unit, and learning as an adventure.

Get to know Kinder and you'll not only like him, you'll love him!

Learn more about Kinder at www.kinderscorner.com.